Scott Morgan is writer of poetry, fiction, and magical philosophy. He currently resides in his hometown of Newton Aycliffe, in the north-east of England.

In loving memory of K.M. and E.M.

Scott Morgan

BALLADS OF LOSS AND WOE

Austin Macauley Publishers
LONDON · CAMBRIDGE · NEW YORK · SHARJAH

Copyright © Scott Morgan 2023

The right of Scott Morgan to be identified as author of this work has been asserted by the author in accordance with sections 77 and 78 of the Copyright, Designs and Patents Act 1988.

All rights reserved. No part of this publication may be reproduced, stored in a retrieval system, or transmitted in any form or by any means, electronic, mechanical, photocopying, recording, or otherwise, without the prior permission of the publishers.

Any person who commits any unauthorised act in relation to this publication may be liable to criminal prosecution and civil claims for damages.

A CIP catalogue record for this title is available from the British Library.

ISBN 9781035816156 (Paperback)
ISBN 9781035816163 (ePub e-book)

www.austinmacauley.com

First Published 2023
Austin Macauley Publishers Ltd®
1 Canada Square
Canary Wharf
London
E14 5AA

Table of Contents

For My Boy	14
Mrs T and the Knights of the Kitchen Table	16
Carbonite	19
There's a Hole in My Heart	21
Spanish Inquisition	22
Ele-Phont	24
Elevenses	25
What's Meg Short For	26
Devastation	28
Why?	30
Bully	32
Alexithymia	37
De Nial	39
All the Things That Could Have Been	41
Sign Language	43
Heathen	44

Panic!	45
Zeitgeist	47
Blue Pilled	48
Puddles	49
Breedbate	50
Revolving Doors	51
Photograph	52
Corkscrew	54
Misery Business	55
Lepers	57
Broken Wing	58
Empty Bed	59
The Curse	60
Gold for the Soul	62
Bitch	64
Whirlwind	65
Druxy	67
The Acorn That Fell Far from the Tree	69
Unknown	71
Airbag	72
Assassin's Creed	73
Tez	74
Dem Blues	75

Exit Stage Left	76
Two Sides of a Coin	77
The Ghost of Christmas Past	78
Sucker Punch	80
A Whisper…	82
Juicy Steak	83
Pillow Talk	84
Life	85
Romeo and Juliet	86
Just Another Love Song	94
I Can See a Liar	96
She Said, She Said	97
Semicolon	98
Scenes from a Movie	99
How Does It Feel?	101
Monsters	102
Wormtongue	104
History Repeats Itself	106
Insomnia	108
A Suicide Note	109
Floyd the Barber	110
Flattened 5th	112
Going to Sleep with Your Socks On	113

Eczema	114
Texas Hold Em	115
A Moral	116
Horse No. 9	117
The Bomb	119
The Life and Times of Sir Tredeguard	120
Left on Unread	129
Marriage Counselling	131
Theres a Word for That…	133
Hangman	134
I'll Never See Your Face Again	135
On the Climbing of Kata-Ranga	136
Amber Warning	138
Era Vulgaris	139
History Is Written by the Victor	140
Temper Tantrums	141
Snapshots	142
What Doesn't Kill You Simply Makes You Stranger	144
Isolation	145
Trouble	146
The Void	148
Teardrops from a Rose	149
The Title That Says It All	150

The Multiverse	151
The Façade Scroll Trilogy Prologue	152
I. An Adventure Riddles in the Dark	153
II. The Battle To the Victor the Spoils	155
III. Aftermath Leave No Trace	156
Naïve	157
Vampyres	158
Tug O War	159
Thank You	160
Pearhead	163
Plastic Bags in the Wind	164
Father	165
The Neighbour from Hell	167
Jack Meadow	168
Shooting Star	171
The Invisible Man	172
God Is in the Rain	174

For
All
The Broken

People change for two reasons
Either their minds have been opened
Or their hearts have been broken

'Trusting people gets you killed…
Loving people gets you hurt…
Being real gets you hated…'

For My Boy

My sweet boy
My baby blue
Heavens arms
Reach out, embracing you

Lay your head down
In eternal peace
Run, fly and love
In your everlasting sleep

Your heart was too big
You felt alone in the world
Solitary and unsure
Your voice would not be heard

If you only knew
How many cared
You might not have left
This world frightened and scared

We will not get to see
You grow year by year
But all of us knew
The good man you were

My daft sweet boy
With love we wish to smother
You left a hole in my heart
From which I will never recover

As we gather here
To say goodbye
To brother, nephew, son and friend
The apple of my eye

We will always remember
Your daft little smile
The good times together
If only for a short while

In our hearts and memories
You now forever reside
With a touch of sadness
But overflowing with joy and pride

So, with love
My little fella
Evanski, my Evan
When I reach my end
I know we will meet again
In Heaven

Mrs T and the Knights of the Kitchen Table

In the early hours, as we travel on the way to our training
Our clothes become soaked, dampened with the raining
We spy the castle-gates, where we could find safe harbour
Within dry sanctuary where we could dis-armour
With haste we clack our coconuts and sally forth
And cross the moat into the fort

The drawbridge is lowered, and we step inside
We bundle indoors with bluster and pride
Divest ourselves of wet and soiled coats
Lady Lisa takes the scroll, reads the notes
Announces our arrival by title and deed
Of all our virtues hereby decreed

First of all. the resident knight, Son of the queen
With the largest of nostrils that all have seen
Brave Sir Pete of the golden dream

Second, we have Sir Rick the hairy
With his quiff on point and head all peary
To rescue many damsels, he deems necessary

Third of the group Sir Scott the virtuous
To keep all in the moment in consensus
For all to be in a state of sensuous

Fourth to enter Sir Ellwood of the teeth
Many foes has he presented with a wreath
His war cry crushes all beneath

Fifth in order Sir Holland of the gringe
Many of freckle and short of fringe
Tiny of stature but large of cringe

Sixth in line comes Sir James
Keep the straight in life his only aim
Keep the group one and the same

Last of all we have the seventh to arrive
Sir Jenkinson the foolhardy, lord of the jive
His musical discs are sure to survive

All announced we take our places around the table of glass
Begin our discussions of what may come to pass
Mrs T takes her place upon the throne, into the mirror stares
The smoke from her berkely floating in the air
Lady Lisa takes her perch beside her and slowly rocks

As Mrs T gently combs and dries her locks
The knights assembled each give their speeches
Unto the queen they make their beseeches
Mrs T listens to each in turn and gives her verdict
The way to ease through the day without conflict

Her platinum blonde hair frames her face
As to each in turn she states her case
All the knights listen with care and patience
To her speech with admirations
All assembled stand and take a bow
For the platinum queen has spoken now

As we ready ourselves for the journey ahead
The words of Mrs T ring in our heads
Furnished with the words from our surrogate mother
Into the bright new day, we set out to discover
What may happen upon our quest
When Mrs T has us blessed

When we return at the journeys end
After a long day questing with friends
With all the energy we are able
We take our places round the table
We are what we came to be
To sit and talk again with Mrs T

Carbonite

When I look upon a picture of your face
Everyone says at your own pace
Frozen in time

When I think of you never growing old
When I gazed upon your form, lifeless, cold
Frozen in time

When I walk into your room, smell stale air
Unable to hear your feet upon the stair
Frozen in time

When I can still hear your voice from behind the door
Yet I know you will never utter a sound, no more
Frozen in time

When I serve four plates instead of five
And realise I will never see your fat belly thrive
Frozen in time

When I hear a song that reminds me of you
All those instances of the goofy things you do
Frozen in time

When I see other people preparing for exams
Looking to the future, readying their plans
Frozen in time

What I wouldn't do to press a button and unfreeze
Breathe warmth into your body and seize
You within my arms; free from the crime
Frozen in time

There's a Hole in My Heart

It
Can
Only
Be
Filled
By
You

Spanish Inquisition

'are you okay?'
Isn't that what they say

'how are you doing?'
Their own construing

'how are you feeling?
Obviously reeling

'how you holding up?'
Just a hiccup

'you'll be alright'
The ends in sight

'anything I can do?'
They gently coo

'I'm here if you need me'
But they mean not really

'It gets easier'
Said with straight demeanour

'it will get better'
From those without fetter

Ele-Phont

A great grey stone which will not yield
Standing silent within the field
What might you know, or may have seen?
Secrets in time which we could glean

Try to dig the depths and excavate
See the truth and carbon date
What was in the past and bring to light
Fill in the gaps and calm our plight

Elevenses

Sit up straight, for you are a lady
Elbows off the table, be bright not shady
Don't talk when your mouth is full
Dribbling food, it makes you look dull
Always practice what you preach
Never take too much, do not leech
Make sure to wear clean underwear
If there's an accident you don't want people to stare
God I'm tired, I'm knacker-jiggered
You must apply rouge, so you don't get triggered
If you walk up the stairs and fart times six
Remember to keep the coffee cakola out of the mix
To drink good tea, from china you must sup
Only then will you get the true flavour within the cup
These are the lessons which I teach
In the future they will be in reach
When I am gone my little flower
You stand tall and never cower
If something you see and you know it sucks
Put your shoulders back and say 'get to fuck'

What's Meg Short For

An Angel appeared from out of the blue yesterday
I had never seen the like before, her visage unsullied
She had a message to bring, of which she had to say
'These snippets in time will leave your mind unsullied'

She opened the book and showed us the story
Moments of joy that had been
Images never seen before in all the glory
Glimpses of another life not seen

She rested a hand upon the shoulder
'These I gift to thee, a reminder of joy
To keep within your heart as you grow older'
To remember the boy

She stood by our side to say farewell
To a former life, now left behind
As the music and tears began to swell
Etched into hearts and mind

A tablet was gifted to hang on the wall
Signed and delivered, hung in sight
Move forward, stand tall
Everything will be alright

As she drifted away, remarked in jest
A question was left, for the answer we beg
She turned and smiled as she said
'What's meg short for?
She's got little legs'

Devastation

I wander through the sun-baked wasteland
Sand crunches underfoot, scathes into my bare feet
The shriek of the vultures circling overhead
Echoes endlessly amidst the cloudless sky
Sunken flesh hangs from my bones
As the sun boils the blood in my veins
I raise a skeletal hand to my eyes
Scan the horizon in all directions
Nothing but desert and the decaying remains of humanity
Litter the barren scorched earth
Crumbling ruins of someone's forgotten life
Has it always been this way?
How did I get here?
I look behind me
Sand dunes haze for miles into the distance
I don't remember
Bewildered, I turn to look in front of me
A mirror image of the vast emptiness behind
No respite
I try to swallow
My throat like sandpaper
My mouth arid, my lips cracked

How long have I wandered?
Has it always been this way?
I set off, a slow shambling shuffle
Any direction as good as another
One foot in front of the other, keep moving forward
There must be a way out of this barrenness
There must be something other than this scorched and blasted earth
A way out
There must be an end to this devastation

Why?

Why?
It's the question on our lips
Into the wandering thought rips
Why?
The unobtainable answer
A song without a dancer
Why?
What was going on
Did we do something wrong
Why?
What did we miss
Little signs did we dismiss
Why?
Is there something we could have done
Put a stop to the end, before it begun
Why?
What did we need to know
Behind the curtain, behind the show
Why?
Would the answers settle the mind
Or bring more questions to find
Why?

Maybe if we knew, we could rewind time
And put a stop to the start, make it fine

Bully

SCENE: *A school courtyard, we see a bunch of girls laughing. Cut to.*

SCENE: *School toilets, the group of girls are stood around. One is writing on the stall door, she reads aloud as she writes.*

GIRL 1: For a free ride, call Ellen on 07754 8364787
GIRL 2: What a slag
GIRL 3: Careful, someone's left a giant turd inside.

All the girls laugh as they leave the toilets.

SCENE: *Classroom*

GIRL 1: Miss, what can you do if you've got really bad BO?
GIRL 2: Yeah Miss, I know this girl and she proper stinks, sweat stains under her pits and everything.

The class giggle gently.

TEACHER: Keeping clean and using toiletries usually helps.

GIRLS 3: But what if you've like, got a stinky fanny Miss.

The class erupts into laughter.

TEACHER: That's enough.

SCENE: *The group of girls are leaving a cinema. Laughing and chatting.*

GIRL 1: Did you see the state of it
GIRL 3: It was gross
GIRL 2: I know right, like something from a nightmare

SCENE: *The bunch of girls are shown in 3 segments, they are sat at home in front of laptops, chatting to each other.*

GIRL 3: What is she wearing?
GIRL 1: Would you wear that?
GIRL 2: I think she looks good

SCENE: *We look down a school corridor outside the toilets. We watch as a cleaner walks down the hall towards, opens the door and steps inside. A few seconds later, we hear a scream. Radioheads 'exit music for a film' begins to play. The cleaner comes out the door and runs down the hall from where she came. We slowly move inside the toilets at floor level, stopping in front of a toilet. After a few seconds we see a girls shoe drop to the floor. Cut to black.*

We see the same scenes play as before, but this time in their entirety.

SCENE: *A school courtyard, we see a bunch of girls, shouting at Ellen.*

GIRL 1: Did you even bother looking in the mirror this morning
GIRL 2: You stink, why don't you go away and die
GIRL 3: Nobody wants you around

All the girls turn and laugh amongst themselves as before.

SCENE: *School toilets, the group of girls are stood around. One is writing on the stall door, she reads aloud as she writes.*

GIRL 1: For a free ride, call Ellen on 07754 8364787
GIRL 2: What a slag
GIRL 3: Careful, someone's left a giant turd inside.

All the girls laugh as the leave the toilets. As they do, we pan over the stall door to see Ellen sat on the toilet, hunched up, sobbing.

SCENE: *Classroom*

GIRL 1: Miss, what can you do if you've got really bad BO?
GIRL 2: Yeah Miss, I know this girl and she proper stinks, sweat stains under her pits and everything.

The class giggle gently.

TEACHER: Keeping clean and using toiletries usually helps.

GIRL 3: But what if you've like, got a stinky fanny Miss.

The class erupts into laughter. Ellen in the back, hangs her head.

TEACHER: That's enough.

SCENE: *Inside the cinema, the girls walk past Ellen, she is carrying a drink and popcorn. One of the girls bumps into her and knocks her food all over the front of her. The girls laugh as they leave the cinema.*

GIRL 1: Did you see the state of it
GIRL 3: It was gross
GIRL 2: I know right, like something from a nightmare

SCENE: *The bunch of girls are shown in 3 segments, they are sat at home in front of laptops, chatting to each other.*

GIRL 3: What is she wearing?
GIRL 1: Would you wear that?
GIRL 2: I think she looks good
GIRL 3: Yeah, for a hippo

The girls smirk and laugh as they type away on their laptops, as Ellen's pc, bings one after the other, with received messages. Ellen sits staring at the screen crying.

SCENE: *Radioheads 'exit music' plays. Early morning, a hunched and dejected Ellen is seen entering the school, walking through the corridors, she enters the toilets, as we stay outside.*

Cut to black. A message reads

THERES ALWAYS MORE TO EVERY STORY

Alexithymia

There are no words I can possibly say
Nor iteration of which I can possibly convey
My feelings are mired in the gloop
I am a fork in a world of soup
I long for a way in which to connect
Speak the words I wish to project
I am impotent, no gushing forth
Weak projections of inner worth

The confusion on people's faces
As my bottom lip stutters, trembles
Unable to speak, only traces
Of meaning meant, which barely resembles
The tumultuous tornado raging inside
Mind to mouth, the connection is denied

Within my heart lonely tears keep falling
My inner voice takes a mauling
Like a beaten child, cower and shrink
Retreat into the foetal position
In an attempt to be succinct
There can be no right decision

If only I could beam my thoughts into your mind
No words are spoken, just two hearts entwined
Understand the sentiments buried within
The sparks of truth that course through my skin

De Nial

There's a boy you've known since he was young
Whom you met when he was introduced to your son
When the two went to see the guardians
They took the thrones they felt like champions
That one simple moment in the past
Remembered well that pleasant task
Of smiling faces and happy feet
The giving of gifts is the greatest treat

Now time has passed, and times have changed
The present has moved, become rearranged
All that remains of that memory behind
Is the one standing in front, the other in the mind
Looking at the good man who stands before
You can see the parallels through the revolving door
As you watch and look into the eyes
You long to support the growth for the rise

Every time you see his face
You wish to support and help him trace
A future that would see him thrive
Give him confidence to take the dive

And forge a great path of his own
To create as he will, and find a home
That is the point of the great masterplan
And to that end you will do all that you can

All the Things That Could Have Been

I close my eyes and drift into a dream
I see you in a room with other teenagers, taking apart
engines while you laugh and joke, the teacher nonchalant
I see you at a party, talking with friends, whilst nervously
glancing across the room at the blonde in the corner, who
every now and again looks your way
I see you sitting on a beach with your wife soaking in the
sun as your young children run with glee towards the ocean
I picture you leaving a bedroom a glow on your face,
holding hands with a beautiful girl
I picture receiving a phone call, you on the other end, exited
yet nervous as you inform me that your fiancé is pregnant
I see you sitting next to your young son as you play video
games as he watches and copies with awe as you explain
what to do
I see you and your wife and children arrive on Christmas day
for dinner, as you say hello and the kids run to nanna
I picture you getting your first apartment, the empty floors
and walls, wondering how you will fill the space
I picture us walking along a sea front talking, you, taller than
me now as we both get older

I see you and your families face as you surround the bed as I take my last breath I can picture you at a job interview, smiling and confident as you charm the pants of them
I watch as your son brings home his new girlfriend to meet you and your wife
I see you learning to drive, too eager, like you think it's a videogame I look over at you as I stand by your side as you nervously wait for your fiancé to walk up the isle
I see you bringing home a dog as a surprise for your children, as their faces beam with joy as you ask them what to call it and they say 'dingus'
I stand proud as punch as you hand me your new-born son and tell me his name 'Leon Scott'
We laugh as your mam and your wife prepare a meal in the kitchen as we sit in the front room playing videogames together
But most of all I picture just turning to look at you as you look back at me and we both smile

Sign Language

We gesture dramatically at each other in silence
Like marionettes with the sound on mute
Our limbs fling about in violence
As desperately we try to commute
And convey what is in our mind
The plainest truths from deep inside
But we are speaking different languages we find
All basic understanding has died
And so resort to grunts and gesticulation
Throw forth random shapes a St. Vitus dance
Moves without a song, no enunciation
All comprehension left up to chance

Heathen

When sweet words are spoken for free
But the ear cannot hear and the eye cannot see
And all that you express to blanket with gold
Is denied at the first; no! rebuked with scold
No empathy for feeling, that is not of oneself
All semblance of understanding left on the shelf
If God himself spoke directly to you
There would be no belief, would not think it true
The trauma that is held deep inside
Wounds of old caused by people who lied
Have severed the connection to the higher
The rod is hollow, vacant of fire
Now all to you is just superstition
Live and sleep in your own perdition

Panic!

Fluorescent blue lights fill the air
Disturbing the calm morning
Penetrate through the windows glare
Making this a blue dawning

Wondering what is going on
There is a thundering on the door
Jump into action, what's wrong
What is this all for

The door swings wide open
Uniformed men march into the house
Not what we were hoping
Nothing we could espouse

There is something outside you don't need to see
Everything fractures, mind spins in turmoil
This isn't possible it cannot be
What was blossomed is now spoiled

A door is opened to an empty space
Realisation hits, as it all becomes real
The blood drains from the face, no sign not a trace
To the heavens make an appeal

As the ground crumbles beneath my feet

Zeitgeist

I woke up one day and looked around me at the world
And I realised that things had changed, new currents unfurled
I looked into people and found hearts and minds had changed
They had lost all purpose; they had become deranged
All the things that we all had in common
Had been dissected, put into a dem-on
A stagnation in one global thought
Lost the soul, instead of doing what everyone aught

Blue Pilled

I am so virtuous, I can discern all wrong think
My heart is pure there is no kink
With my collective we seek out the roots of evil
Purge the individual with righteous upheaval
With my mob of zealots, patrol the airwaves of science and thought
Remove all those not behaving as they aught
We have eyes and ears always alert
To patrol your mind and dig up dirt
No-thing will pollute our perfect order
We follow the rules of the warder
Like workers bees in synchronicity
Our hive will be made sweet, wholesome and free
Shame! Shame! Shame! Is our holy chant
Empty vessels into which our lords decant
The scriptures of our new world
To guide us as the way unfurled

Puddles

When you wake up face down in a puddle
And you're drenched from head to toe
Don't get yourself in all of a muddle
Just roll over and let it all go

Throw a towel down to cover the mishap
It will dry up and be forgotten, pay no mind
No need to fret or get yourself in a flap
No discourse needed or to be unkind

Perfectly normal, there's no need to fix
A silly little mistake
Most would understand the risks
Empathise and appreciate

And if it should ever happen again
Don't fret or fear others frothing
disregard what is in the brain
Carry on as if it was nothing

Breedbate

Always looking for the angle you need
To turn the conversation towards your creed
There is no patience for understanding
Only one outcome that you are demanding
The words that emanate from others lips
Are just an opportunity for you to flip
Peaceful connections into consternation
Crumple the smooth with defamation
Transpose the words onto your level
Create the mixture in which you revel
Your divine dance of hate and love
Only one way do you desire to shove
All intent to twist the knife
Fashion the storm and bluster with strife
To create the pain on which you feed
Like a junkie to fulfil that need
The pleasure you imbibe from the pain
Serves your addiction to the insane

Revolving Doors

I wander aimlessly opening door after door
Searching for something, what am I looking for
A thing lost, but once I had in hand
I've forgotten what it was. I don't understand
I look straight ahead but never behind
In the future is the thing I need to find

Hoping against hope with each portal opened
The vision will appear, and life awakened
Endlessly in an eternal loop
Of missing links and Freudian hoops
Aborted births of the mother
Have left the corridors empty, I discover
It once was in front of me, where it belonged
It must be here somewhere, where has it gone

Photograph

As time trickles on and all things change
The faces you remember fade become estranged
Turn into a glimpse, not a complete picture
A pinch of salt within the mixture

All of those times you never paid attention
Assuming there would be no need for retention
To a smile or laugh, insignificant at the time
Recede into the recesses of the mind

Staring at a picture, was it real, a dream?
Losing all sense, somewhere in between
If you stare hard enough, it might make it real
Regain some clarity, all the confusion repeal

Faces remembered, disappear and rearrange
Become blurred and forgotten snippets estranged
The only way to reignite the feeling lost
Restart the heart, dispel the frost

Memories fade and become forgotten
All in time like the apple that is rotten
Attempting to make the empty visible
Staring at a picture trying to drink in every pixel

The only instance that is left to see
A mosaic of postcard memories
Those things now only exist in pictures past
Sate the itch and break the fast

All that remains, a snapshot of time
Emblazoned within your heart, faded in your mind
Signposts of a time now past
Of the moments you assumed would ever-last.

Corkscrew

There is a corkscrew impaled within my chest
The pain I am in defies all comprehension
It twists its way deeper, forces closer to my heart
I grasp the handle, try to stop the piercing pain
Pull it from me; it just hurts as much
It hurts going in, it tears to take out
This torment is unbearable
Trapped in limbo of anguish
I weep forth a torrent of blood red tears
For my insides are a broken bottle of wine

Misery Business

You're in the business of misery, and business is good
Creating the demand like any good peddler should
Withhold the product until the time is right
Then deliver a sample to ease the plight
Lure them in with a gentle caress
Provide a taste with which to impress
When euphoria permeates the very core
The hooks are in and you know they want more
Shut up shop and make them wait
The willingness to loyalty, do anything to placate
Send round the boys to keep them in line
Spout forth a darkness on which to dine
When they are cowered and cornered beaten down
Left feeling like they are going to drown
In you swoop with a balm of love
Ease the hurt with your silken glove
Take away all the pain and hurt
Forget the sorrow, those feelings subvert
Float naive and free in the garden of pleasure
A glimpse of the gift of which you should treasure
You leave them alone solitary and cold
When purchase is sought make judgement with scold

With pleading for reward make them give thanks
Zero dissidence Confine with the branks
When conformity is gained customer assured
All pretence is dropped they have been cured

Lepers

Walking down the street the alarm in my head begins to ring
All the people I encounter appear strange and unconvincing
What is it that unnerves them so
Why do they stand apart with social distancing

As I journey along all stare
Like they have no with which to compare
The pod people point and whisper
He is different from us of him beware

Forced by the world into a room of one
Wonder what could have gone wrong
Why are you singled out
Why don't you belong

Infected with a disease of the heart and mind
Others shun and disavow; you are not their kind
They don't want what you have got
What it's like to be you they don't want to find

Broken Wing

My wing is broken I cannot fly
No matter how many times I try
I stretch and strain the broken bone
But cannot make the movement come
Hampered by the constant crush
Told not to try, not to push
Let it heal, give it time
Reinforced by constant rhyme
But I must stand, I must take flight
I cannot wallow in this plight
I have to try, even if I fall
Rather than never try at all

Empty Bed

Standing and staring at the empty bed
Small creases litter the quilt like scars
Fading evidence of slumbers past
When it was a deep abyss of shelter from the day
A small indent on the pillow
Where a head full of hopes and fears
Once gently lay
A hand slowly caresses the sheet
Cold to the touch
Breathe in
No scent lingers
Deserted. Not in use
A relic
A fossil
Devoid of life
Just a remembrance of what used to be
An empty bed

The Curse

There were three brothers, large of heart
Set out on a journey from homesteads hearth
To seek out fortune, to seek out life
Full of optimism, free from strife

They wandered long and travelled far
Saw many things, took many a scar
Until one day when all changed
Fate stepped in and rearranged

After fourscore years a tragedy untimed
One of the brothers fell behind
The oldest was hit by a car and choked
His journey ended, his life revoked

At first sadness took their thoughts
How could they go on one man short
Life is full of uncertainty
They pledged to go for posterity

So, on they went for many a year
Pleasant journey Smooth and clear
Nothing did perturb their soul
As they headed onward to the goal

Life went on bountiful and free
As all blossomed pleasantly
Everything seemed to take its course
No need to worry or remorse

All of a sudden, a storm raged
Battered all with wind and wave
The youngest became entangled in rope
Pulled to the depths without hope

Only the middle was left
Solitary, alone, utterly bereft
Severed from the past, no future destination
A lone wanderer in segregation

Was this a punishment? Was this a curse?
Natures joke, cruel and perverse
Was it some unknown sin
Wondering would it come for him

Gold for the Soul

Gazing into the abyss, is there something there?
A vast expanse, a thousand universes to behold
There is nothing in the world to which it can compare
You would sell your soul, for a glint of this gold

You could know all that happens simultaneously
Instant gratification, no need for delay
Like mercury intravenously
When you throw yourself into the fray

Truly connect with others of your kind
See what was once beyond comprehension
Ultimate knowledge beamed into your mind
A lightning bolt to kickstart your ascension

No one will know, it will be a secret for you only
This power that you gain
Will be held safe within, internally
A locked safe with a secret flame

All of your heart's desires may be found
The sweetest high and the purest rush
The deepest thoughts that you'd never sound
A gentle finger against the lips…shhh…hush

Oh! this vibrant web, this myriad of wonder
A heavenly surge of justification
Imprint the heart and longingly ponder
All connect in unification

Bitch

Better watch out this bitch is in heat
Her ears pricked up, she's light on her feet
Her emotions are channelled, blood on the rise
Someone is lucky and in for a surprise
Tattooed form reveals its own story
When you see her in all her glory
She'll roll onto her back and let you rub her belly
Feast all you want at the open deli
When she's had her fill and is fully sated
She loses a howl, entirely appreciated
But beware this bitch! Her teeth are concealed
When you are not aware, all will be revealed
Her bite swift, sudden, sharp
Confusing, lost in the Larp
You will be left helpless, at her mercy, her prey
A cold lifeless corpse, nothing left to say

Whirlwind

Lying to my face again
With suicidal innocence
Playing for the game
Imbecilic decadence
Loose your bullets
In the hope one hits
Push and pull it
Tear until it splits

Narcissistic drama queen
Stamp your foot until the earth quakes
Dissipate a broken dream
Until you thrive within the flakes
Gyrate the world until you're dizzy
Nothing left still or serene
Don't look now keep it busy
Nothing heard, nothing seen

Lying to your face again
With fake dissidence
Sabotaging all the same
With wicked confidence
Twisting the knife
Blood streams
The end of life
The end of scene

Druxy

Take the branch from the tree
Soft and smooth to the touch
Moulded, like it was made for thee

Measured, will make the perfect crutch
O thy lord, blessed be!
This is all too much

The days are long
And the night never-ends
Journey in fool song

No thought it is all pretend
Never imagined it was wrong
Never noticed the staff bend

For years journeyed
Believed it was support
But within was envied

Faux was the rapport
And the form became heavy'd
The bond became taut

No-one to grasp, none to catch
Reach for the bough
It breaks and snaps

Fall to the floor, ow
Reality seeps in through the cracks
Everything turns grey somehow

This staff of gold
This worker of dreams
Not was foretold

Rotten to the seams
The bough that was sold
Weakest of beams

Tumble to the floor
Raise eyes to the sky
Have been left poor

Cry aloud why!
There is none truer
Was it all a lie!

The Acorn That Fell Far from the Tree

Why do special people change?
The twists and turn life takes are strange
Standing alone at breaking dawn asking why?

Flummoxed, Stunned, no idea at all
When did you fumble, when did it fall
When did it rot, wither and die?

Someday you will leave me
Crushed beneath a landslide
In a sun-baked barren wasteland, with my throat dry

Wake up, breathe, don't you cry
Dreamed a dream, it was just a lullaby
So wipe that tear away from your eye

Flummoxed, Stunned, no idea at all
When did you fumble, when did it fall
When did it rot, wither and die?

Someday you will leave me
Crushed beneath a landslide
In a sun-baked barren wasteland, with my throat dry

If people believed in words, there in for a bummer
You said you and I would never die
Until the world stops spinning and we joined the sky

Why! Why? Why?

Unknown

Half my life
I lived within a dream
Cracks began to appear
Things not what they seem
Picked at the corner
Pulled back
To take a look
Saw the fields of bodies
The clank of meat hook

Airbag

Was it foolish, or was it naïve
Openly wear my heart on my sleeve
To think a heart and mind
Would be alike, in kind
Never to imagine a possible betrayal
Or foreseen a will to fail
Untruths spoken direct to face
No guilt, void of disgrace
Taken as law, set in stone
No reason to doubt, a message from home
You were steering the car, chosen destination
I was left afar, still at the station
I was just in the passenger seat
No airbag in front, the ground at my feet
Reach your stop, slam on the brakes
Windscreen meets face, a thousand mistakes
Smash into the concrete and wither deflated
As you continue your journey, proud and elated

Assassin's Creed

Everything is permitted, nothing is true
Manipulate, leave your clue
Manoeuvre, carve your path
Anticipate the aftermath

Ravish your ego, take their due
All will follow, the plan you drew
Enclosed within the maze, mystery of you

Tez

A walk somewhere, can't think why
A small group, young, dumb and spry
When Tez regales us with a little story
All the details, in all its glory
About what went on the night before
And why the little head was mighty sore
'I plunged in and went for broke
But all too soon, hit the vinegar stroke
I noticed that she wasn't flowing
So, I thought, fuck it, just keep going
After pounding away for eternity
I ran out of steam, had to leave be
She wasn't impressed, with pouty face
I never got started, nor finish the race
Bloody hell lass I'll tell your plight
It was like sticking my dick out the window and fucking the night!

Dem Blues

Yes I'm lonely!
Wanna die!
Yes ii'mm lonely!
Wanna diee!

As I sit and think about the myriad humans
That bluster and roam across this garden in space
Colliding, sparking and repelling
Never stopping to connect, nor delve beneath the surface
And what it would take for them to stop and look
At the amazing twinkles that reside within the eternal brook

Yeees iiimm looonellyy!
Wanna die!
Iiimm lonely!
Wanna diiee!

And I wonder, when stars become separated and solitary
They have no constellation, to reflect the art
Develop as black holes, vacuous to themselves and space
The perpetual cycle of which we are a part
It is gravity that connect us, gravity that defines us! Apply!
Brothers! Sisters! wake up and fill the night sky

Exit Stage Left

Non-one sees the rehearsal
They just see the performance
Those who create their own drama
Collect their own karma
The truth will out

Two Sides of a Coin

The difference between us?
I was building a house.
You were just sheltering from the storm.

The Ghost of Christmas Past

No echoing of cheer
No smile from ear to ear
No creak upon the stair
No presents upon the chair

No bite into the pie
No sleep encrusted eye
No stocking on the bed
No relative over fed

No annoying uncle fester
No children playing jester
No smell upon the stove
No revealed treasure trove

No delight, joy or glee
No socks for me
No smile alights the face
No life left in this place

Just shadow and silence
What is left at last
Just the absence of life
Ghosts of Christmas past

Sucker Punch

Heading towards the final rounds
Confident almost assured and sound
All of a sudden…whack…the fatal one, two!
Knocks you off your feet, tears your mind askew

World spins around you a kaleidoscopic blur
Deafened by the buzz, a crackling silent whir
Knees fracture and disappear, gravity calls
There is no ground, to catch your fall

Tumble everlasting through a void of pain
Branded reality will never be the same
Try to regain focus, reach out to feel
Lost amidst the waves, a ship rolling full keel

A count heard faintly, the din of the crowd
But your brain is fractured, over eyes a shroud
Lost at sea with no sight of land
Treading the waves, screaming for a hand

All diminishes as your head goes under
And the world as you knew it torn asunder
When you open your eyes, to pastures strange and new
Everything is different, the strange thing is you

A Whisper...

I hear...

A faint whisper on the wind...

It whistles my name...

I turn to look

But it is gone

Juicy Steak

If you sit and think about the gist of it all
There are those that may stumble and those who fall
But who sets the bar and who makes the call
Who is the arbiter of the great enthral

What is the point, what is the end goal
Who are you? The spark, the soul?
Why are you here? What is your role?
What is the thing that gives you control?

Pillow Talk

I cuddle a cold pillow at night
And I think
I can warm you
But you can't warm me

Life

Yes
No
...
No
...yes
Yes
...yes.
Yes...

No
...no...
Yes
No
yes.
...
No
...
...
...
Okay

Romeo and Juliet

"For never was a story of more woe
Than this of Juliet and her Romeo."

Scene: *inside a church, the chapel, Juliets slumbering body lay atop an altar covered with s shroud, the chapel is dimly lit candles flame all around. Romeo bursts through the doors and into the chapel.*

ROMEO: say not in despair, I shout thy name, aloud I declare, Juliet say it cannot be true, where is my love? where are you?

He sees her laid upon the altar.

ROMEO: (*stumbling forward*) O! my love, what has befell thee? What calamity has taken you from me?

He falls in front of Juliet's prone body.

ROMEO: my sweet, great love of my life! What is the cause behind all this strife!

Paris enters the room.

PARIS: what is going on here! Who are you? Where is my woman, where is my boo?

ROMEO: this is your fault! What have you done? Why is Juliets life unspun?

PARIS: who is the interloper? The so called Romeo? Why are you here? When did you grow?
What have you done to Juliet? Tell me now, for that is my threat!

ROMEO: I would not harm one hair of her head, I arrived here to find her lifeless, dead. 'Twas you who did her wrong, filthy dog, spill your song!

PARIS: I have not seen her since last night, when she did grace my bed with sordid sight!

ROMEO: say it cannot be believed, of that union perceived

PARIS: believe it true, she has no match, her chin against my sack did scratch!

Romeo feels sick to the pit of his stomach, thinking of the two of them together.

ROMEO: sweet Juliet, it cannot be true! Why! Did our love mean nothing to you!

Romeo slowly walks to the altar.

ROMEO: while you spoke of love and future plans, in secret trysts, my mind you did scam. You played a game of give and take, of dark deception for your egos sake?

Romeo reaches the altar, resting his hands against it, his head bowed, as the deception sinks in. he turns to look upon Juliets face.

ROMEO: (*seeing the beauty he so loves*) Why? Why would you give yourself to him? Why would you shame me with your sin?

Paris begins chuckling quietly behind him.

PARIS: she was never yours, unsighted fool. It was just your turn, simply a tool. Love-bombed with promise sincerely made, and shows of affection fondly displayed. You were simply a means to an end, a lump of clay for her will to bend.

Romeo turns to look at Paris.

ROMEO: I believed in her words, delightful and true, my heart with joy they did imbue. Of how we were soulmates, destined to join, of how our love was two sides of a coin.

PARIS: there's no such thing as love, only on TV, she needs a stronger shove, tis why she ran to me.

Romeos face hardens, his anger rising.

ROMEO: the trickery with her wiles, the duplicity behind her smiles. All the time wrapped in your arms, with scorn and laughter, I fell for her charms. She deceived that much is true, was she led astray because of you?

PARIS: your naivety is boundless, my beta friend, you act as if there's honour to defend. You play the game without knowing the rule, unbeknown to you, you're simply the mule!

Parid hubris grows as he laughs at Romeo.

PARIS: you're not a man, any women would want, she seeks for value to fill her font, the mirage is such for which you care, yet she runs to me to pull her hair!

Romeo rages.

ROMEO: you mock me with your caustic words, to belittle me by throwing turds. If so high and mighty you are, why are you eager to feather and tar?

PARIS: because you are a useless cuck, to survive thus far, must have taken some luck!

Romeo slowly reaches behind him a pulls a knife from his pocket.

ROMEO: you preach of alpha, yet I see you are beta inside, let us cut you open and see what you hide!
Romeo screams and lunges at Paris, who easily sidesteps, parries and swings the blade back at him, plunging it into

Romeo's stomach. Romeo looks down in shock at the knife protruding from his stomach as he falls to his knees.

PARIS: and here we have an important lesson, there is no control, there is no possession.

He crouches down to look Romeo in the eye.

PARIS: it's okay, don't be afraid to cry, I'll give your regards to her whispering eye.

Romeo dies with a gasp. Paris stands. As he turns to find Juliet stood in front of him. She plunges a knife into his stomach. Parsi looks at her and looks down puzzled.

JULIET: what's wrong my lover, are you not glad to see? Is it not your turn to be impaled by me!

Paris stumbles over.

PARIS: we could have been rich you stupid…b…i…tch.

JULIET: I am Me! I do not need either of you. Not your pomp and not his twee. With this seed inside I will take my place, within your house, showered with dignity and grace.

She pulls the knife out of his stomach, causing him to cough blood. She starts to walk over to Romeo but is interrupted.

PARIS: Jul…(*cough*)…Juliet…(*cough*). watch out… for… Rollo Tomassy…

Paris keels over dead. Juliet walks over to Romeo and places the knife in his hand. She takes a phone from her pocket and dials.

JULIET: (acting hysterical) Hector! Help me! Theres been a fight! They are dead!
They're both dead!
I'm frightened and alone unsure where to tread!

Hector: calm down, tell me where you are. I know the place it's not too far.

Juliet hangs up and returns to her calm demeanour. She sits on a bench and readies herself.
Sometime later, hector and his men burst through the door and into the room.

HECTOR: what has happened here? What has transpired? What is the situation in which you are mired?

Hector sees the bodies of Paris and Romeo slumped on the ground.

JULIET: O! thank the gods you are here! Bewildered I am and crawling with fear!

HECTOR: (*bending down to touch his son*) Paris my boy, what has befell thee? What fatal event has taken you from me?

He stands and grabs Juliet's arms.

HECTOR: tell me what has happened to my son! Tell me this thing that was done!

JULIET: (*acting distressed*) we were sat relaxing, talking of our plans, when Romeo burst in brandishing a knife in his hands. He attacked without word and swung for a cut, Paris protected me and took one to the gut. Before he fell, he got one back, he pulled out a blade with a swift attack, and stuck it into Romeo, ending him with a killing blow.

HECTOR: hush my child, just you rest, I will sort, take care of this mess

JULIET: (*resting a hand on her belly*) we are safe thanks to your son, we would not be, if this thing had he not done.

Hector looks down to Juliet's belly in recognition.

JULIET: your son maybe dead but he is not gone, a part of him will forever live on.

Juliet smiles at Hector, who nods back. Placing his arm around her shoulders, he guides her towards the doors.

JULIET: tell me, dear Hector, if I'm being too sassy, but do you know someone named Rollo Tomassy?

Hector's face turns to stone for a moment, recognising the name.

HECTOR: I do not recognise the name, discard it from your brain.

They exit.

END.

Just Another Love Song

What is this thing called Love?
Which so perturbs men's minds
Complicated web Arachne wove
Within the darkness blinds

Seeks to spin eternal sting
The precious, eternal white light
Siren song does all men bring
Entangled in their plight

Upon silken beds lay
Fed upon sweet nectar
Cut off supply, obey!
That whispering spectre

Emaciated with a satient glow
Yet withered, plundered and worn
Discard into the pool below
A quest to be reborn

What is this thing called love?
Which so perturbs men's minds
Unknown force persistently shoves
Towards the beast who dines

I Can See a Liar

I can see a liar
With hair the colour of fire
Yet eyes like a glacier
You'll never see it coming
No warning bell will sound
Forced overboard
Sink or swim
Believed and bought the ticket
Been left exposed
By the worst kind of liar

She Said, She Said

She said all the things you wanted to hear
She told you of your greatest fear
She spoke of all the things to come
She informed you of the prize you'd won
She wove a tale, a prize so fair
She asked why aren't you like them over there
She said you're the only one I trust
She spoke to others because 'she' must
She said we can live on love alone
She spoke in secret on her phone
She spoke the vow 'forever be'
She said 'you can go now, I want to be free'

Semicolon

When you see the world on a different level through the use of one good eye And you watch others run around chasing how what when and why
Your heart and mind burn with the thought. Why am I different?
Why do people act the way they do, everything is insufficient
They have two good eyes with which to see
And yet are blind and full of misery
Do I join the matrix and follow the herd
With only one good eye could never fit in, that would be absurd

Scenes from a Movie

My eyes used to follow you around the room
A thing beyond my control
The most amazing thing in the world to me
Pure gold to the soul

I longed to be alone with you
And taste those strawberry lips
To awaken with the rising sun
The fire still on your hips

A picture by the riverside
Laughing as you pull a stupid pose
The wrinkles that form around your eyes
As I boop you on the doze

I watch you digging in the garden
As you skin glistens in the sun
Composing words for a sonnet
Of the magick yet to come

Falling asleep on the couch
I'm not tired you demand
Five minutes later, I take you to bed
As I lead you by the hand

Walking in to find you
Painting the hall
You've got more paint upon your self
Than on the wall

I watch you smile with nova eye
As I slowly close the door
Trying to prolong that final click
Knowing that I will never see your face no more

For when I enter a room again
Cold dull and pointless, your directors edit
You will not be there to look upon
Just a fade to the end credits

How Does It Feel?

How does it feel like, to lose a thing most precious?
Your soul becomes fractured, like a jigsaw missing a piece,
it will never be whole again.

How do you move forward from that?
You don't. you're alone. There is no forward.

How do you cope with the ultimate betrayal?
Reality is shattered and all becomes exposed. Nature shows
her true self.

How is it to have your story told by others in Chinese
whispers?
Like watching a movie you know the end to

How does it feel to find out it was all a lie?
Like turning up to school without any clothes on.

How does it feel like to be in your shoes?
How does it feel to know, that no-one would find your body
for months?

Monsters

There are monsters that whisper in my ear
Pointing out all the prevalent fear
Of what has been and what may come
And of all the ways you could be undone

They show what lurks behind the eye
The motivation for which they vie
The secrets in the hearts of man
The machinations of the hidden plan

They tell you there is no truth
In sweetest word or harsh uncouth
No worry and no care for you
No penny for what you do

They whisper that you're all alone
You have no-one to call a home
You are not worthy of others time
Existence is just a crime

In solitary confinement you hear them talk
And you fight, you do your best to balk
But all you have is the monsters and the night
And the more they whisper, the more they are right

Wormtongue

Don't worry you're in control
Take back that beautiful soul
You can act your own role
I'll help you reach the goal

You do not need that soothing hug
Nor warming feeling when you snug
Swat away like a troublesome bug
Just dust the room, shake the rug

Steer your new course down the river
Hold your hand, fill your quiver
I'll be there, don't you shiver
You have what you need, you're the giver

Change the name
Get rid of the pain
You can be sane
A family once again

I'll tell you the truth, trust in me
Nothing holding you back don't you see
You can be what you want to be
My advice, be footloose and fancy free

History Repeats Itself

history repeats itself
torch passed on from one to another
history repeats itself
with glad tidings, dirty nappies upon the shelf
history repeats itself
daddy left its plain to see
history repeats itself
mammy will look after and nourish thee
history repeats itself
the wall is built, you are protected
history repeats itself
remain pure and never infected
history repeats itself
mammy will keep you under her wing
history repeats itself
she will always tend to your broken wing
history repeats itself
you are strong, you don't need anyone
history repeats itself
everyone else is wrong
history repeats itself
siblings painted with the same brush

history repeats itself
nothing to see, hush, hush
history repeats itself

Insomnia

Sleep Eternal

O! glorious respite
Float amidst the sea of night
To shelter from the incessant day
A plague of daggers, stab and bay
Hound the marrow, crush the bone
Hunched under the cover, all alone
The truth slithers into the mind
Half hoped dreams, never find
Bloodshot eyes, dry, no tears
No reprieve from the hounding fears
How to stop and shut it out
Cannot rail or scream or shout
Amidst this noise, never a word
Everyone's talking, yet no one heard
Bare feet grace the freezing floor
In solemn silence through the open door
The gut twists with creeping dread
The only hope amongst the dead

A Suicide Note

Floyd the Barber

Standing in front of the mirror, twins laugh
At how to deal with the aftermath
If you move in the wrong direction
You'll be left with a sore inspection

I teach how to deal with Pedro's lip
Slow and smooth; 'I am' you quip
I giggle to myself at the concentration
As you carve yourself in expectation

I stand and watch as a father stoic
As you try your best to be heroic
You do the best to follow the lead
To trim the growth and cut the weed

I watch a little man try to be big
As too hard into your face you dig
'ouch' you note as you nick you chin
'I cannot do this, I cannot win'

You're to clumsy and with a lack of patience
You chirp out in that fluctuating cadence
I can't do this, I can't go on
Just get me an electric one

Flattened 5th

With heavy heart and mind perturbed
He sits alone on his hill undisturbed
And he plays his lute a solemn song
His thoughts his own to sing along
Notes drift out to a silent crowd
He does not care for he is not proud
He sings his ballad of loss and woe
For the blues are his alone to know

Going to Sleep with Your Socks On

No gently warming caress on the back of the neck
Nor whispered dream sounds in the dark
Limbs entwined, an impossible maze
Replaced with crumbs of yesterday's breakfast
The sheets stink of beige
Smell of summer fruits long since dwindled
Nothing to spoon
Just the foetal position, the only warmth left beneath an ice scorched quilt

Eczema

Every moment that niggling itch
The scab is calling you. Pick at me
You fight valiantly, to be somewhere else, someone else
The hand moves involuntary, hidden desires to know
Just
A gentle rub
A piece snaps off. A jolt of pain shoots pleasantly through the mind
Violently tear to expose to the sun
As a trickle of blood. Flows. The winners champagne
Fresh wound. Victory achieved

Texas Hold Em

People don't abandon people they love…
They abandon people they were using.

A Moral

A solitary sparrow is flying south for the winter, trying to find some respite, a place to call home. On its journey it falls into trouble, the frost and the chill, makes its way into the single bird's bones and it freezes and falls to the ground. A cow walks along the road where the sparrow is frozen and as it walks past, it shit's on the path, covering the sparrow; then continues on its journey. The sparrow warmed by this happy accident begins to thaw, to warm up, to regain its life. It feels the blood pumping through its veins. Just as the sparrow is beginning to gain its senses, a cat walks by; finding a serendipitous gem, the cat cleans away the manure and devours the sparrow before it can react.

Everyone who shits on you is not necessarily your enemy.
Everyone who gets you out of shit is not necessarily your friend.

Horse No. 9

Walking through a crowd of downturned faces
No one looks, yet everyone stares
Placing accumulators one each other's races
Who the losers are? They do not care

The buzzer sounds, it's all a go
Some of them don't even start
The bravado was all for show
Couldn't tell the living and infirm apart

Some crash and fall at the first few hurdles
A mess of bodies soon forgotten
As the race moves on, insides curdled
Left behind and rotten

As the pack is thinning, frontrunners emerge
Butterflies flap their wings through the veins
No one looks up, they just further submerge
This could be the moment, the start of the reign

Heading to the finish more fall behind and falter
Only the favourites are left in the running
Many a Dreams sinking in the water
Scramble for the heels in their cunning

The final few, with whip and gritted teeth
Strain to edge the nose in the fore
There can be only one winner's wreath
Only one name written in lore

The finish line crossed, there is no peer
Arms aloft, jump for joy; waiting for praise, yet
There was no one left to cheer
There was no one left to bet

The Bomb

The charred remains of a thousand souls litter the scorched earth
Dog hairs on a carpet of blackened grass
All is silent
Even God has vacated
Smoke and steam intermingle, slowly rising
A signal flair
Stay away, something dreadful has transpired here
Carrion circle overhead, savouring the time, choosing the plunder
Amidst all this catastrophic waste
Within this carnage
The larvae of a million maggots reach out
Snaking tendrils breach the surface
Swarms of fly's buzz to each other
Come, embrace the spoils, take your fill
No humanity remains within medusas garden
It is no place for such things
Just rotting flesh and the smell of a thousand charred hearts

The Life and Times of Sir Tredeguard

I.

Bequeathed into the world
On a crisp November morn
Through the door to life
Sir Tredeguard was born

With eyes of purest ice blue
Hair, a wisp of wheat brown
Slight of form, clean and new
Swaddled in a fresh babes' gown

His mum did swoon and sway
All buoyant with joy
As she held in her arms that day
The most sweet baby boy

His father with smile, and joy
The gods answer the call
They have gifted a boy
With biggest of ball

They cuddled and cooed
With love and awe
The new addition to the brood
A life without flaw

He was spirited home
To lay in his castle
Walls of black stone
Keep him safe from hassle

Introduced to the family
The circle was complete
They cuddled him calmly
'isn't he sweet'

His sisters though small
With delight did smother
Love Him with all
Their new little brother

II.

As a babe he settled into life
He chuckled, with hearty laugh
Free from all strife
The easiest of path

The day came when he took first steps
An easy affair
As good as it gets
Waddled across the room without a care

He received his first steed
A tiny little thing
Would build up some speed
As the song would ring

His days and nights were spent at play
Full of freedom and fun
A new adventure every day
Of deeds to be done

III.

Soon it was time for school
To mix with others
Who acted all cool
And vexed with their bothers

Within the group he saw the truth
Opportunity never missed
Speak his mind even though it be uncouth
Told the teacher 'He smells of piss'

The rigmarole was not for him
Pointless and tiring
He lived for the win
In the chair ready and firing

IV.

As a deadly disease ravaged the land
The family hid
It did not go as planned

His father fell ill, slipped into a coma
All were worried it could be bad
Father might not see the dawn
Contagion overtook him mad
Rendered weak and shorn

When Tredegar was stricken ill
Joined his father at rest
Unholy quiet upon the hill
No time for play or jest

As he and his father lay in limbo
Twins asleep in bed
With symptoms akimbo
One foot in the land of the dead

For 4 days and four nights
He lay deep in a coma
As his body tried to fight
And resist the corona

When to the rescue came the physician
Presented the miracle cure
It was an easy decision
Of that the family made sure

V.

Although he was left weakened
By the ravages of disease
He started his training

Took to it with ease
Resting in the day
And working at night
He learned how to play
Obtained the skills to fight

With sword and gun
And acrobatic skill
Magick in his veins
Words bend to his will

After years of practice
He felt himself ready
To test himself, hit or miss
Forthright and steady

The time came to receive his prize
Presented before him
On opening the box, he showed surprise
The weapons of a knight within

As he raised sword aloft
He face alight with bliss
Armed, ready and strong
'I fucking love this'

VI.

He became chained
At a great celebration
Sought out queens to free

A great view for emancipation
As the damsels looked upon him
He flapped his smile
A disarming grin
Pleasant view won with guile

As he wandered through valley and hills
He found many a demon littered the land
Darkness within, spreading hurt and ills
Duplicities wherever they ran

It became clear he had to fight
To sow virtue and banish
Trample the evil with all his might
Free the land from this tyranny

He journeyed to the secret place
Where the fabled treasure was hidden within
Hunting for the clues
The secret he could win

Armed with zombie protection
He battled through the horde
No damage taken, all deflection
As he put all the to the sword

He reached the centre of the maze
Stone statue of a maiden fair
Fell upon his gaze
Entranced with her stare

He found the switches to unlock
The curse upon her laid
Squeezed the button beneath her frock
And fell into his arms

VII.

The secret of the red pill found
He knew what he must do
Into his new training was bound
To learn the secrets of kung fu

As his skills in VR began to grow
The code began to clear
He began to understand, to know
What lurks beneath the veneer

He hacked into the matrix
A universe of possibility
Run jump fly for kicks
Freedom from triviality

VIII.

One day by chance
Across a lonely room
His eyes caught in a glance
The reflection of the moon

He was smitten from the first
With her fantastic mind
They would quench each other's thirst
They were two of a kind

Their days on walks
And their nights dining
Long drawn out talks
Treasure mining

In their magical kingdom
They blossomed their own world
Block by block
Their perfection was unfurled

She gifted him a scarf of red
A symbol of their heart
Words never said
But never be apart

IX.

As he lay in bed one night
The army of the dead attacked
Surrounded the castle to fight
The witch queens voice blacked

The armies surrounded his castle gates
She led them in the back door
To try and seal his fate

To pervert his inner core
With pitchfork and cursing flame
With burning crosses and noose
They shouted his aloud his name
Verbal volleys let loose

He knew that all was lost
The rot had entered the castle
Fireplaces covered with frost
The family become vassalled

X.

Solemnly he gathered his things
Took one last look around
Whatever the future may bring
His name would not be found

He lowered the castle gates
Looked upon the army gathered
He would not bow to fate
His soul never battered

He mounted his horse
charged out to meet them
his sword raised high in the air
he screamed out 'freedom!'

Left on Unread

I'm sorry for the things that I couldn't fix
To make it smooth and warm for you
I had no idea of the worries in the mix
Of the discomforts making your heart blue

I wish you were here to hear my voice
I would spend the rest of time in your ear
I would guide you to a better choice
And swat away all of those fears

Talk to me, tell me about your day
Do no fret over other's games
I am here a constant midst the affray
I can soothe and ease the pains

I was supposed to improve and make better
To point you to the sun
All I had was an empty letter
The scroll of life undone

The sorrow was not yours alone to bear
I would have taken the weight on both shoulder
But the fault is mine for not making you aware
I was there, for you, to help embolder

I wish that there was still a charge left
Open the app, find all the messages new
I would not be so bereft
Of just how much I loved you

Marriage Counselling

I'm sat in my lonely room
Dreaming of you
The fact that I still need you
Is a constant source of consternation
The angel and devil upon my shoulder
Constantly bicker, back and forth
There is no middle ground
Both right and both wrong
The truth is somewhere in between
Simmering anger never allowed to vent
Thrown to the wolves without a say
A story written by caprice
Booted straight into grief
Never given a chance by anyone
I still need you?
But I don't want you
I want you to experience
The shoe on the other foot
Would you behave the same?
Of course not
So I let them fight
At least they are communicating

And with time will come understanding
Knowing that the truth
Came from my love, from within myself
But not from the shadows of your deception

Theres a Word for That...

When you started comparing me to others
Instead of comparing others to me
You revealed your true nature
Hypergamy

Hangman

I _ _ n't

_ v _ r

L   o _ _ d

A

M   _ n

_ h _

W _ _

T _ _ t

I

L _ _ e

_ o _

I'll Never See Your Face Again

As each long day, begins and ends; gets left behind
With new events and moments with which to bind
There are some sunbursts which do not rise
No treasure house of images on which to feast the eyes
Just faded portraits of masters past
An account of history that cannot last
The only evidence remains in the one who give'd
Of events and flashes and what was lived
Longed for time which never will return
But in the heart and mind forever burn
I watch and stare at the passing throng
But never find the thing for which I long
The multitude of facades that rush past the door
I know I will never see your face no more

On the Climbing of Kata-Ranga

The extreme places I have been to, the extreme places I have known
I had to up give up everything and take it on all alone
Shivered on the mountain crag
The shrieking blizzard tries to drag
The warmth from within my soul
And replace it with the cold

The arduous journey I have took, unto long and dizzying heights
The shadows in the fog and the demons I had to fight
Stripped me down and left me bare
Alone at the mercy of the beast's lair
No starlight left to see
No way of breaking free

I had to stand and climb for this
I had to live then die for this

I had to leave anything and everything that could help me at all

To struggle to the summit alone, whether I stumbled or I might fall
Battered, scarred and bruised
Running in the night pursued
The secret within my heart
That I carried from the start

I would give my life for this
I would die a million times for this

Amber Warning

All is at peace, smiles and laughter fill the air
No disturbance perturbs, the actors all debonair

The icy blue sky begins to shrink with the imposing gloom
As a thick dark cloud seeps in and begins to clog the room

The words once pleasurable and bountiful with joy
Take a turn for the worst, as the spider begins to toy

The siren song begins in the faintest recesses of the mind
A warning sound; the triggering of the force unkind

The signs are clear, this storm has been born many times before
The ride rough; wake up shipwrecked on the shore

Nothing can be done, there is no way to avoid the ineffable
Just batten down the hatches, grit the teeth, steel for the inevitable

Era Vulgaris

Stand on any street corner and take a look around
the Aeon of the Child is everywhere found
dummies on the concrete, covered with dirt
not even a penknife amongst, with which to be girt
smash the patriarchy, down with capitalism
daddy buy me the new iPhone to tweet my outrage
what is a woman? The riddle of our times
mother's milk is from a bottle, not from the divine
discontent and disconnected wander the ghostly earth
barren of meaning for which to divine the worth

temet nosce

History Is Written by the Victor

I was an analogue watch in your digital life
Outdated and not needed for the midlife
Your social presence is a reflection of the sun
One look behind the mirror and it would all be undone
But with no-one to say; not to hold you to account
You can present an image without having to dismount
The truth has been hidden, buried and not spoken
Of what is within you damaged and broken

Just one psychological drama one after the other
There is no shame with which you have to bother
When you lose all of the battles, but win the war
Free to write the history of what you were fighting for
The story told is one of heartache, triumph against diversity
Of how you survived against the evil adversary
Propaganda which you spew, convinces all of your picture
The history is cemented, as is written by the victor

Temper Tantrums

Lie

Lie to my face

Call me a disgrace

While you laugh off all your mistakes

Lie

All pretence of grace and beauty vanished

Only vitriol your ego furnished

Lost truth until tarnished

Lie

When on-one around

You might be found

Lie

Web of deceit you are

Bound accountability

To yourself escape

Your ego a victim screaming

Of rape

Never another point to be made

Snapshots

I think of you rolling on the floor, tears streaming from your eyes
Because I've just farted in your mouth and its 'NuCleAR, there is nO HopE!'
I laugh as I hear 'fkin cheatin bstard' among many other cries
As a voice answers back 'I'll wash your mouth with soap.'

My eyes all intent as you talk of the recent game you've just won
Which means nothing to me, but means the world to you
Then I place my arm on your shoulder, tickle your side 'that's my son'
As we both laugh; because we both understand the due

I hold you as a new-born within my giants arms
With your tiny feet; so many adventures to walk
Your bright blue eyes ensnare me with your charms
As I rain down kisses upon your forehead. SWALK.

Your days at school in the uniform of red
Tattooing your arms with ink and rolling in the dirt
As you come home tired, hungry; ready for bed
You ask for your favourite 'got any noodles' you assert

Opening your presents on that Christmas day
With the wisest and funniest words you have mastered
There is only one thing which you wish to say
'this is the best ever, I fuckin love this bastard'

As I sit half asleep on the couch, eyes heavy at two in the morning
As you run and jump from couch to couch; playing assassin
With a tiredness tinged with childish joy, I play games till the dawning
Even through exhaustion, we roleplay with a passion

I stroke my palm across your frozen cheek
The scarf around your neck not enough to keep you warm
There is no life for my fingers to seek
I failed to keep you safe from harm

What Doesn't Kill You Simply Makes You Stranger

The vault is opened
The treasure laid bare
All for the taking
Smile at partner
'we did it'
A kiss
The knife is thrust
Straight into the gut
'why'
'I kill the driver'

Isolation

Sat in silence, no voice permeates the room
A deafening echo hiding amidst the gloom
The walls are currently caving in

The world outside the window
Surrealistic landscape flow
No idea to bring out from within

Stranded on a different planet earth
I am the alien, I have no worth
And I'm running out of oxygen

Eyes look down instead of up
Defence against the corrupt
No more scars upon the skin

Cower between the magnolia walls
Hide from the shout, conceal from the calls
And I shrink amidst the din

No people to betray the fear
No one to hold dear
So, I sit and sob in isolation

Trouble

I never meant to cause you trouble
I never meant to cause you pain
I tried to splendify your bubble
Instead, you drove yourself insane

I poured forth love to fill your cup
Full to the brim, overflowing
Fermented into poison, which you sup
Corruption set in, unknowing

Your light became darkened
And you fell into the abyss
Your ego damaged and disheartened
Whispered you were missing out on bliss

So, the holy sanctity destroyed
Turn your back upon the truth
All the things with which you toyed
The mirrored reflection soothed

Now there is no number for you
Construct a house of rubble
Tell a tale of any hue
You will have no trouble

The Void

Awaken each morning to a cold lifeless sound
No movement detected, no presence is found
No light persists within the dimmed room
Nor glimmer of hope sparks amidst the gloom

Teardrops from a Rose

Is a rose still as beautiful at night?
With no thing around to catch the sight
No bee alights the fragrant petal
Nor scarlet blanket on which to settle

Fade to black amidst the night
No living colour without the light
The sun that makes visible the pumping vein
Has descended into sleep again

Silken limbs curl and retreat
Fearful of the dark, of deceit
A cocoon refuge, petrified of the dark
Hastens the light coming, seeks the hark

As dawn peeks over the green horizon
The dewdrops fall to greet the rising
Little tears shed for the coming sun
Has survived without being undone

The Title That Says It All

WHEN YOU BREAK UP THE BAND AFTER 25 YEARS CITING CREATIVE DIFFERENCES, AND SIX MONTHS LATER YOU'RE IN A NEW BAND, WITH SOMEONE YOU WERE PLAYING SECRET SHOWS WITH, SIX MONTHS BEFORE

The Multiverse

I cannot help and look to the sun
And think on all the things I won
I cannot help but feel the frost
And reminisce on all the things I lost

In the howling wind I find
The beauty from within my mind
I cannot cover from the sting of rain
Each icy drop reminds of the pain

Of all the things that came to be
From choices that were made by me
A different person on a different plane
A different outcome might change the game

Something became from the random choice
Something unique, with a unique voice
But to lose such a treasure, nightmares enthral
Is it better to not have such a thing at all?

The Façade Scroll Trilogy
Prologue

With all deceit and duplicity laid bare
You are unable to claim the eye with a stare
For if you were to look for too long
Reminder of all the things you've done
When darkness meets the light
You have to make false fight
All the guilt and shame you hold
Mirrored back at you threefold

I

An Adventure
Riddles in the Dark

Need alone time
Bang the drum
In thought crime
Having fun
Riddles in the dark
Seeking answers
Wait for the hark
Multitude of chancers
Tingle in the mind
Dangerous game
In secret to bind
Fleeting fame
Another day
Need a fix
Want to lay
Use the tricks
Start melee

Thrown in jail
Alone to play
Don't want bail

II
The Battle
To the Victor the Spoils

Alone amidst the heat of the battle
One on one, blab and prattle
Each word a barb shot into skin
Say anything to seal the win
A phrase with warmth, a term so cold
Each statement pronounced in bold
Subdue the target at any cost
Will not be the one who lost
As the final killing blow is landed
The loser on their knees, left stranded
Rewarded with the spoils, the treasure
To bask and glory in the pleasure

III
Aftermath
Leave No Trace

Everyone who has seen or has heard
Isolate and make them look absurd
If they might converse with the prisoner
Hear the story, be a good listener
Brand them as a traitor to all
Remove the power to make the call
Separate them from the sphere of play
So there can be no interference in any way
Control the narrative of the bubble
Everyone will fall in line without any trouble
Be free to continue without any shame
For at the feet of another lies the blame

Naïve

You can laugh and claim that I'm naïve
That I see the best, easy to deceive
But from the hope in my heart, no reprieve
This I know

People with the plans and schemes
Only show you what they deem
Theres always more than it seems
All for show

Well, I pity those that hide in secret
Feel the need to lie and cheat, it
Must be terrible to live in fear
Reap what you sow

But to see the world through the lens of love
Well, that fits me like a glove
So, I smile with happiness from above
And let it flow

Vampyres

Beware the monsters who lurk in plain sight
In their human form they scour the night
With silken words they bend the ear
Flatter you with all the words you wish to hear
Smile and play until your distracted
From the sinister way in which they acted
Weakened you succumb and follow their lead
Never notice the pin prick from which you bleed
The pleasure washes over and you feel elated
They have you hooked until they are sated
Fulfilled they lay you down to sleep
Into the bliss you fall in deep
But when you awaken to the morning sun
Drained, without the strength to carry on
Never occurs, what actually happened
Just a killer hangover, the mind flattened

Tug O War

One side pulls to take the prize in their arms
The other simply resists to prevent a victory

Thank You

Thank you.
For all the lessons I learnt
For all the fun at the beginning; at the end all the hurt

Thank you.
For teaching me of lust.
When you'd start an argument, so you could hide in secret in the other room on your phone; for you that was just.

Thank you.
For teaching me of jealousy.
When you'd smash my phone off the wall if I stood within 10ft of a woman, to you a heresy

Thank you.
For showing me the vow.
When you lost your wedding ring and your phone on the same day somehow.

Thank you.
For teaching me about caring.
When two weeks after my diagnosis, you never bothered to ask and I had to do the sharing.

Thank you.
For the lesson on peace.
For all the worried sleepless nights, while you slumbered in deep.

Thank you.
For the lesson on winning.
Whilst I dance to your tune, oblivious to what you were planning.

Thank you.
For teaching me the truth.
That I thought you were adult but you wanted to recapture youth.

Thank you.
For learning me of deception.
Whilst you lived your double life and clouded my perception.

Thank you.
For the lesson on honesty
Sweet words whispered, a disguise for your frivolity.

Thank you.
For the lesson on lies
What was really going on disguised by your cries

Thank you
For the lesson on narcissism
Where you love bombed me and forced into a Schism

Thank you
For teaching me how to leave
To reveal your true self and show me what you deceived

Thank you
For showing your sins
All the different stories you told while you post all your wins

Thank you.
For showing me the way
For leeching me dry and throwing me away.
To be reborn and thrive another day

Thank you.

Pearhead

It's a Friday night and you're looking all debonair
With a 70's chest and the slick quiff in your hair
The boys are all gathered, with a need to get kicks
It's time for you to do your thing and pull your tricks
Walk into the store and flash your grin
Walk out with a bag full, all the boys yell 'win!'
Go hang in the park, decide what to drink
You choose the clan dew, all yours to sink
Regale us with tales of your 6th this week
You're in love again and hath slain the cheek
Turn to the left with you Zoolander pout
'my ice cream makes the girls scream and shout!'

Plastic Bags in the Wind

Battered and bruised, smacked from pillar to post
Unable to find a grip on the thing you need the most
To seek to grasp on the solid ground
The fiercest wind mutes out any sound
A glance to the heavens to see if they heard
There is no recognition, that would be absurd
Whipped to the side, snagged on a twig
Rips open a wound, flap like stuck pig
But gravity will not let it be
Pulled in two directions, there is a struggle to break free
Fly off into the twisting air
As the world around moves by without care
The looping gust throws into a new direction
Unexpected, unprepared; cannot find the inflection
If it was possible we would all rescind
For everything is just a plastic bag at the mercy of the wind

Father

There is no need to fill your heart with worry
Or sting with the bitter pang of loss
There is no reason to be sorry
Do not sour your mind and be cross
It was nothing you did, or what was said
A thing beyond your control
What was playing the movie in my head
I wish I could have told you, but you wouldn't understand
You would have spoken words of wisdom
That would not have changed what was planned
I just want you know the heartbreak that you feel
Is not because of what you have lost
But because the love you hold for me inside was real
I'm so sorry that I had to leave so soon
And leave you on your own
I did not mean to cause you grief and rob you of your home
There is no blame to be laid upon you
For there was reason behind the madness
All things must come to an end, start anew

You will find happiness amongst the sadness
For I am always here to talk to you, I'm always by your side
From the moment of creation, until the time I died
The fact you are my father, was always my greatest pride

The Neighbour from Hell

I could hear the words through the paper-thin wall
When you thought no-one was listening at all
As you talked and made your plans

I was informed you had been seen from afar
When you were spotted sitting in your parked car
Back when it all began

I had to listen to the crocodile cries
And all the frustrated sighs
As you vented to the man

I used to cover my ears from all the fake fights
But I could see it all in plain sight
I knew you never gave a damn

I felt myself cowered with the shame
As I had been involved in the playing of the game
And told you, you should of ran

Jack Meadow

THE TALE OF A MOST UN-EXTRAORDINARY FELLOW

Jack's eyes flipped open to the buzzing of his alarm clock. Jumping out from the comfort of his cocoon into the cold morning, he slapped his palm against the clock, restoring peace. Trudging downstairs into the silence, he flipped the kettle onto boil for his morning coffee. The only sound to disturb his one-bedroom apartment, the gently growing hiss of boiling water.

*

He stood in front of the sink staring blankly at his reflection in the mirror. Not handsome, nor ugly. An average face for an average man. His clean-shaven face, topped with short dark hair and finished off with light blue eyes, features, unremarkable. Looking down at the lone toothbrush perched atop the counter, he picked up the toothpaste and squeezed out a pea sized amount and began to brush his teeth.

*

At the supermarket, an old woman hobbled past him, with a pile of groceries precariously perched on top of her trolley. A box of cereal fell to the floor. She struggled to bend down to pick it up. Jack strolled over and picked it up off the floor and replaced it atop her trolley.

'Thank you dear' she croaked 'it gets so hard these days.'

Jack smiled at her and took his place in the queue. He waited patiently as he watched the checkout assistant gossip with the woman she was serving.

'See you, have a good day,'

He stepped forward. She smiled a tight-lipped smile and put her head down to scan his groceries.

'Cash or card?' she enquired nonchalantly.

'Card,' jack replied. The scanner beeped as he held his card against it. The cashier began to serve the nest customer as jack picked up his shopping and left.

*

Jack sat in the canteen, quietly eating a cheese sandwich. He looked around at all of his work colleagues hunched over tables, some of whose names he didn't know; even more he had never spoken to. Each one eyes wide, faces glued to the screens of their phones. Turning around to look behind him revealed the same vista. The house was full, but nobody was home.

*

He stood watching the microwave revolve. His reflection in the glass door mixed with the meal inside. The low droning noise filled his head, as he watched the numbers slowly count down. The chicken dinner within gradually cooking, its sizzling intensified, until the bell rang and it was done.

*

He stood on the side of the road looking left and right, waiting for the traffic to subside. Glancing across the other side, he saw Nicola and a group of her friends were deep in conversation, their smiles wide but their topic inaudible. He had a crush on Nicola for years but never had the courage to do anything about it, nor had she indicated any interest in him beyond polite conversation.

As they crossed in the middle of the road, he looked directly at her and smiled.

'Alright, Nic,'

Too locked in conversation, she didn't notice or respond. He lowered his head and moved on.

'Oh! Hey Jack,' Nicola's voice from over his shoulder snapped him from his reverie.

He stopped and turned. Nicola was stood smiling at him.

'Do you...'

A car slammed into him, sending him flying into the air and over the bonnet. Jack crashed to the concrete with a thud as the car sped off.

As he lay on the concrete his body broken, gurgling blood, his eyes roamed across the crowd. Some stood in shock, hands covering their mouths. Others were frantically tapping away on phones. Surrounded by people, yet all alone.

No-one came near.

Shooting Star

I look to the sky
In the hope you catch my eye
But the black sea is devoid
All waypoints destroyed
And yet I try

I sigh with a wish
That it will not diminish
But there is no colour in the sea
All light has ceased to be
The darkness full of anguish

I hope with my heart
It was not a thing apart
Was it just imagined?
The event is quarantined
No idea where to start

The Invisible Man

I.

The crowd has gathered and the scene has been set
the people take their places decked out in red
awaiting the queen for the go-ahead
to make show of the honour and clear the debt

the speech is began, spoken with fervour, read aloud
all fall into silence as they stare transfixed
at the queen in the centre, her halo, kissed
not a dry eye remains amongst the crowd

she does the rounds, meeting and greeting
in the moment of darkness, she shines so bright
as they bow in supplication, to the shining light
for the gift of the moment, even though it was fleeting

II.

The multitude has arrived for the long goodbye
As the queen in her horse and carriage arrive
Showered with flowers upon which she thrives
They long for an audience, they scream, and they cry

The music begins as the party's take their seats
The master of ceremonies gives the speeches
As heads are bowed, to the lord beseeches
Until the queen stands last, and regales with her feats

As the chambers are left, amongst the throng begins to mingle
She glides around the room and receives her glory
Everyone wants a piece of her story
She regales them all with her tales bilingual

God Is in the Rain

Do not look upon my image and cry
I am not there, for I did not die
I am the clouds that swell with the coming rain
I am the teardrop that trickles down the windowpane
I am the gentle lap of waves against the shore
The seed nestled at the heart of every spore
The wind that whispers to the leaves
Gentle laughter carried on summers breeze
Butterfly flitting from flower to flower
The passing of the stars as they mark the hour
The morning sun as it roars into life
The long-held hug between man and wife
I once was there and will be again
When the fields thirst, God is in the rain
So do not think on me and cry
I am forever inside, I did not die

Printed in the USA
CPSIA information can be obtained
at www.ICGtesting.com
LVHW020451021223
765241LV00088B/3029